My First Animal Library

Armadillos

by Cari Meister

Bullfrog Books

Ideas for Parents and Teachers

Bullfrog Books let children practice reading informational text at the earliest reading levels. Repetition, familiar words, and photo labels support early readers.

Before Reading

- Discuss the cover photo. What does it tell them?
- Look at the picture glossary together. Read and discuss the words.

Read the Book

- "Walk" through the book and look at the photos. Let the child ask questions. Point out the photo labels.
- Read the book to the child, or have him or her read independently.

After Reading

- Prompt the child to think more. Ask: Have you ever seen an armadillo? What other animals have body armor?

Bullfrog Books are published by Jump!
5357 Penn Avenue South
Minneapolis, MN 55419
www.jumplibrary.com

Library of Congress Cataloging-in-Publication Data

Names: Meister, Cari, author.
Title: Armadillos / by Cari Meister.
Description: Minneapolis, MN : Jump!, Inc., 2018.
Series: My first animal library | Audience: Ages 5–8. | Audience: K to grade 3. | Includes index.
Identifiers: LCCN 2017041708 (print)
LCCN 2017039082 (ebook)
ISBN 9781624967498 (ebook)
ISBN 9781624967481 (hardcover : alk. paper)
Subjects: LCSH: Armadillos—Juvenile literature.
Classification: LCC QL737.E23 (print) | LCC QL737.E23 M45 2019 (ebook) | DDC 599.3/12—dc23
LC record available at https://lccn.loc.gov/2017041708

Editor: Jenna Trnka
Book Designer: Leah Sanders

Photo Credits: Torugo/Adobe Stock, cover; erniedecker/iStock, 1; Heiko Kiera/Shutterstock, 3; leekris/Adobe Stock, 4; Wayne Lynch/Getty, 5, 23bl; Arto Hakola/Shutterstock, 6–7; Animals Animals/National Geographic, 8–9, 23tl; Joe McDonald/Getty, 10–11; Tim Zurowski/Getty, 12; David Cutts/Alamy, 13; Bianca Lavies/Getty, 14–15, 19; schankz/Shutterstock, 15; Steve Bower/Shutterstock, 16–17, 23tr; Matt Knoth/Shutterstock, 18; Norbert Wu/Minden Pictures/National Geographic, 20–21, 23br; Joel Sartore/Getty, 22; lalito/Shutterstock, 24.

Printed in the United States of America at Corporate Graphics in North Mankato, Minnesota.

Table of Contents

A Good Digger

An armadillo digs.

Look at its long claws!

They are sharp.

He has a long snout.

It moves the dirt.

What is he doing?
Making a burrow!

burrow

He sleeps in his
burrow all day.

He wakes up at night.

Then he will hunt.

See his small eyes?
He does not see well.

How does he find food?

He smells it!

He smells ants.

His tongue
is sticky.

It is long.

It eats ants.

An armadillo is covered in plates.

They are made of bone.

They protect its body.

plate

Oh, no!

A coyote!

It wants to eat the armadillo.

The armadillo jumps in the air.

Wow!

The coyote is surprised.
The armadillo runs away.
He is safe in the burrow.

Parts of an Armadillo

plates
Plates cover and protect an armadillo's head, legs, back, and tail.

ears
Medium-sized ears help armadillos hear well.

tail
An armadillo's tail helps it balance.

claws
Long, sharp claws help armadillos dig.

eyes
Armadillos have small eyes and cannot see well.

Picture Glossary

burrow
A hole or underground home that an animal lives in.

plates
Smooth, flat pieces of armor on an armadillo's body.

claws
Sharp and curved nails on the toes of an animal.

snout
An animal's long nose.

Index

To Learn More

Learning more is as easy as 1, 2, 3.

1) Go to www.factsurfer.com
2) Enter "armadillos" into the search box.
3) Click the "Surf" button to see a list of websites.

With factsurfer.com, finding more information is just a click away.